P9-DUD-295

Stories I Forgot to Tell You

DOROTHY GALLAGHER

nyrb **New York Review Books** New York

This is a New York Review Book

published by The New York Review of Books

435 Hudson Street, New York, NY 10014

www.nyrb.com

The following chapters have previously appeared, in slightly different form, as follows: "Yalta" in *The Kenyon Review*; "Ballerina," "Mea Culpa," "Julie," and "Bones" in *Epoch*.

Library of Congress Cataloging-in-Publication Data
Names: Gallagher, Dorothy, author.
Title: Stories I forgot to tell you / Dorothy Gallagher.
Description: New York : New York Review Books, 2020.
Identifiers: LCCN 2020004666 (print) | LCCN 2020004667
    (ebook) | ISBN 9781681374802 (hardcover) | ISBN
    9781681374819 (ebook)
Subjects: LCSH: Gallagher, Dorothy. | Authors, American—
    20th century—Biography. | Sonnenberg, Ben. | Editors—
    United States—Biography. | Multiple sclerosis—Patients—
    United States—Biography.
Classification: LCC PS3557.A4115547 Z46 2020 (print) |
    LCC PS3557.A4115547 (ebook) | DDC 818/.5409 [B]—dc23
LC record available at https://lccn.loc.gov/2020004666
LC ebook record available at https://lccn.loc.gov/2020004667

ISBN 978-1-68137-480-2
Available as an electronic book; ISBN 978-1-68137-481-9

Printed in the United States of America on acid-free paper.

10 9 8 7 6 5 4 3 2 1

For Ben, after all

When I was a young girl,
well I had me a cowboy....

—JOHN PRINE

Contents

Preface

BEN DIED SUDDENLY on a sunny June morning in 2010. When October came I sold the apartment where we had lived for the thirty years of our marriage, urged our elderly cat into her carrier, and moved us a few blocks away, into the fourth-floor walk-up studio that had been my office.

In the months before Ben's death I had begun research for a book, a biography. Now I went back to it: from early morning until early afternoon I immersed myself in someone else's life. The remaining hours of the days and nights were dark with grief, but the time I spent on the book was a respite. I was so grateful to have work to do.

Inevitably, the day came when the book was finished: the last line had been written, the copyediting completed, the proofs read. Still, every morning I walked across the room to my typing chair. Not to write, just to sit in the chair awhile. For almost forty years my working day had begun in one typing chair or another. In the early years I sat in front of a manual typewriter with a sheet of paper in the roller; later at an electric typewriter, then a computer. To sit in front of a writing instrument, to edit, to write, was the habit of a lifetime; more than a habit, an addiction. Those were hours when even the pain of a toothache would recede. I thought only of the work before me, full of inflated confidence that sooner or later I would be able to solve the problems it presented. I'm sure the Buddhists have a word for it.

It was never my intention to write about marriage, widowhood, and grief. Grief is grief, no life is immune to it, and many widows have spilled their guts on the subject. But I found that when I was alone I was talking to Ben all the time. I told him what I was doing, what I was thinking; I told him stories about the things that had happened since he died; I recalled the years before I knew him; I described the new apartment I had found; I told him about the death of our cat; I reminisced about our lives; I reminded him of a yellow bathrobe I used to wear; I re-argued old arguments, brought up old grievances; I apologized for this and that, and for that and that too; I spoke about our friends: who was still living, who had died, who had drifted out of my life. Five years passed and I was still talking to him. One snowy February morning, since I was sitting in my typing chair anyway, I began to type.

Yalta

TELL ME THIS: Do you think that in the years since you died my life has continued as before? Do you think that I still walk through our rooms, that my clothes hang in the closets, our pictures crowd the walls, the bookcases are crammed full, all our belongings remain in place? Do you imagine that when evening comes I light the lamps and our friends gather?

No, none of that. I'm not there anymore. Almost everything is gone—sold or given away. When I closed the front door for the last time the rooms were empty, the shelves and walls were bare, not a clue to our life remained. Strangers walk through those rooms now. They look through the windows at the sun setting over the Hudson, they invite their friends to make merry, they think our apartment belongs to them.

Shall I tell you where I live now? In two rooms that

would fit into our old dining room. No, don't worry. You haven't left me in penury. I live in a penthouse, I have a terrace, the sky is all around, I look out at Central Park at the pond where weeping willows grow, I see across to Fifth Avenue where the buildings glow like fire in the setting sun.

I found this place a year after you died. At first I thought, No, too small; then I remembered: I live alone now. That first hot summer I grew tomatoes in planters and cosmos in pots. Mockingbirds built a nest on the rooftop. They sang all day long and hatched babies that grew big enough to flap into my open door. One day I saw a hawk hovering, the next morning there was no birdsong.

For a long time after I moved here I felt a mistake had been made, as if I'd gotten on the wrong bus and ended up in someone else's life. Every day I sent you an email, the same message each time: Wish you were here wish you were here wish you were here. Sometimes I called our old telephone number and stayed on the line, trying to hear something in the silence.

I've grown used to silence, I live without voices or footfalls. Sometimes a siren shrieks on the street below, sometimes the telephone rings, but most of the time

I hear only the ringing in my ears and the refrigerator cycling on and off. And the wind: how it howls up here on the seventeenth floor! But then comes a day like today, in the middle of February, when there is no breath of wind. The sky is solid pewter, snow is hanging in the air like a gauze curtain, the buildings across the park look like a painted set behind a scrim. And, if you'll believe it, two mourning doves are huddled on the terrace rail.

Didn't I tell you to be careful? "Don't catch my cold," I said. Wasn't that dumb? *I* was the careless one, and you were at my mercy. Maybe I leaned over to kiss you, we shared a fork, I coughed. Sure enough, a few mornings later my cold sniffled in your nose, by nighttime it rattled in your chest, by morning you were laboring for breath. It was only a cold; a bad cold, yes, but you'd had colds before. What could happen on that perfect, sunny June morning?

I came back from the drug store with the antibiotic. I made you some tea with honey and lemon. Just for a moment I looked down to read the instruction label on the pill bottle. I looked up. To see *what*? Your mouth slackly open, a dark stream of tea spilling down your chin. And your brown eyes, lighter and clearer than the tea, wide open, staring at *nothing*. Life gone! In the blink of an eye! While I was *talking* to you! Were you still in the room? Did you hear me scream your name?

I know, I know. We talked about it often enough. When death came, I was to let it be, you were to die when you died. We didn't think to reckon on panic. And so it all happened as we agreed it would not: the frantic 911 call, the medics, the chest compressions, the respirator, the ambulance racing to the hospital, the ICU where you lay for six days, on a ventilator, sedated into coma, except for a few minutes every now and then when you rose to consciousness, when, during one of those moments, I asked you: "Do you love me?" And you, who couldn't speak for the tubes down your throat and the oxygen mask on your face, flashed your eyebrows three times. Like Groucho Marx. I took that as yes. What if I'd asked: "Do you forgive me?"

Sometimes I think about a horror story I read long ago. On a moonless winter night a poor miller and his wife sit by the fireside in their cottage. They are grieving for their only son, accidentally killed by falling into his father's threshing machine. Suddenly a genie material-izes. He offers to grant the parents one wish. Naturally, they wish to have their son restored to life. Very well, says the genie, and vanishes in a puff of smoke. Soon there is a knock at the door of the cottage. Joyfully the miller and his wife fling open the door. There stands their son, his body mangled and dripping with blood, just as he had been in the last moment of his life.

What's the meaning of that story? Never trust a genie? No one gets the better of death? But just let the genie appear to me and I'd give him a try. I'd ask that you be restored to *sentient* life for an hour, even half an hour. I'd specify a date: Friday, June 11, 2010, when the calendar I've kept from that last year shows me that we were alone in the apartment. I'd specify a time, five o'clock in the afternoon, when the sun inclines over New Jersey, making the river sparkle like fireworks, and you wake up from your nap.

An ordinary afternoon then, except that I seem to be starting a cold. We're in the bedroom as we usually are at that hour: you in bed, me sitting at the table between the windows. You've had a two-hour nap but you're still tired; you're always tired these days. Your voice is so weak that I lean forward to hear you. What did we talk about on that actual afternoon? I can't remember, nothing important: What happened today... who called...what will I cook for dinner. But on this day that the genie has granted us we'll have no idle chat. We know what will happen: we know that our time together is coming to an end; that in seven days, just as I'm reading to you from the label on the container of the pills meant to cure you, you will die of the virus that is showing its first symptoms in me today. Do you see what I've asked the genie for? Not so much. Everything. Just a few minutes when we can say goodbye.

So we'll talk about our life together, and about illness, the elephant in our ointment. You're marrying a cripple, you said to me in our earliest days. Do you remember what I said? "Oh please," I said, "don't romanticize yourself, you're not a cripple, you're diseased." We laughed, but at what? After all, you were no less a cripple for being made so by multiple sclerosis, a disease famous for its inexorable crippling effects, a disease with no cure, barely any mitigating treatment, really nothing to be done. A stranger might well have asked: *What* is she thinking? More to the point, What *isn't* she thinking?

Not about the years to come, as you progressed, so to speak, from one to two canes, to a walker, to a scooter, to a wheelchair you could still wheel, and finally, when you no longer had the use of your arms, to a wheelchair controlled by your increasingly hard-won breath: from paraplegia to quadriplegia. No, I wasn't thinking about any of that. Certainly not about incontinence, catheters, bedsores, or about the sudden, middle-of-the-night crises of illness that would occur not infrequently. Nor about my father's question to me when he first met you: "What did he do in his good days?" *So* like Daddy! But what did *he* know? *I* knew that *these* were your good days, the days when we began our life together.

Call it a failure of imagination, call it denial, call it perversity. I saw my life with you, it didn't matter that any fool could see where you were headed. Remember that man in the restaurant? It must have been on a late summer day; we were on our way home from the farmer's market on Columbus, with corn and peaches and tomatoes and zucchini piled into the basket of your scooter. We stopped on Broadway, at Teacher's for lunch. (I know you had a hamburger; every time we went to Teacher's you had a hamburger.) The man walked past our table. He stopped. "How much is the corn?" he asked. He was speaking to you. I was puzzled. Why would he want to know how much you had paid for corn? Then I got it.

He wanted to know how much the cripple, hawking vegetables from his cart, was charging for corn.

So if I wasn't thinking about illness and the upshot of illness, what *was* I thinking? I was thinking of the astonishing luck of our meeting. We weren't children, we'd had lives: four unraveled marriages between us, not to mention the broken love affairs, or the hysterectomy that had put paid to a possibility that time was taking care of anyway. And, you: Two decades of sowing wild oats on two continents on your father's money; my rake, my dandy, my *flâneur*, my bad boy, a dabbler in poetry and the theater in his bespoke suits and hand-cobbled shoes. But also my autodidact, reading *everything*, longing for acceptance as an *homme sérieux*, begetting three daughters along the way. And then, the first symptoms of the crippling disease. Weren't we the very definition of damaged goods? If I was in denial I took my cue from you, who were not the least bit humbled by, who barely deigned to notice that you'd had a bit of bad luck. Was it courage or arrogance? A happy combination of both? If that's what people call denial, what's wrong with it?

And, in fact, *pace* Daddy, years of good days *were* ahead. If we had come to each other late in life, we had also come late to serious ambition, which made us feel young in possibilities. I was in the midst of research for a book that would be my education; you were on the verge of publishing the first issue of *Grand Street*, which would turn out to be a literary triumph: "One of the great literary magazines of the postwar era ..." and so on; praise from your first issue to your last. If going out into the world became more difficult for you, no matter; the world was eager to cross our threshold. So many dinners, so many parties, it seems to me I was shopping and cooking all the time. And so, after all, what better moment could we have chosen to begin our life together? Illness had its uses for you: it steadied you with limits, it made you sit down.

Of course, as my mother liked to say, to live life is not always to walk through a meadow. No. And this is what I want to say to you: As the disease consumed more and more of you, I was sometimes in despair, sometimes felt drowned by the demands of illness, sometimes filled with rage. You knew that. But did you know that there was never a moment that I regretted our marriage, never a moment when I didn't know how impoverished my life would have been without you? My sweet boy, let me add this: Crippled as you were, diseased as you were, the time never came when you lost your power to charm and seduce. You could make me jealous. You knew that.

And you? You'll tell me that sometimes you hated me for your dependence on me, for my impatience, for my sharp tongue, for the times I stalked out of a room knowing you couldn't follow. I knew that. But tell me that you trusted me, that you were proud of me, that we had good times, that I made you laugh.

You used to say: "Remember that weekend we went to Massachusetts and you got pregnant with Harry?" So amusing. So true. Harry was our boy. I picked him from a litter in Florence, Massachusetts, and presented you with the dog of your life. How you loved him! Your shade, wherever it is, loves him still. Sometimes I measure our years by the lives of our animals—eleven years of Harry, followed by seventeen years of Daisy (poor little creature: she never measured up) running concurrently with nineteen years of Bones, an entirely satisfactory cat. A two-dog-one-cat marriage. Actually, a marriage three dogs long if you count yourself. "I'm just an old dog," you used to say…"give an old dog your paw…give an old dog a pat."

I've had my last marriage and my last dog. These days it's enough for me to talk to dogs I pass on the street.

"Hey, doggy," I say; if he's doing his business, I say, "Good dog." If he looks at me and wags his tail, I give a pat. And when I see an old dog, with a grizzled muzzle and arthritic limp, a dog whose days are almost done, I think of the poem Lucia wrote for you:

> My friend said: Write about the dog in *The Odyssey*—
> four hundred pages in. I found him lying on a
>   dung-heap
> where ticks sipped his blood . . .
> And I wondered if my friend had played a trick—
> setting me up with this dog who does not do
>   anything but die . . .
> I wonder
> if he would have liked to remain
> for another line or two, if only to thump his tail.

I wondered too. During that last week as you lay comatose in the ICU I wondered what you would wish me to wish for.

Remember the summer we went to Sag Harbor? You rode your scooter around the town, Harry trotting at your side. "This place reminds me of Yalta," you said. Yalta. Of course. Why not? And ever after, when we talked about that vacation, we spoke of our two weeks in Yalta. Listen my boy, I haven't gone soft in the head: Dead is dead, I know that. But where does that leave me? If not you, who will ever know that once I summered in Yalta?

Snow

So often these days I find myself thinking about things. Not lofty things, just *things*—objects, stuff. Things I have, things I had, things that once belonged to other people that are now mine by default, things I've given away, things that have vanished into the ether. Early in my life my mother noticed that I coveted the goods of this world. She saw a flaw in my character. "They're only things, darling," she'd say, "they're not important." I thought then that hers was surely the proper, more elevated perspective. These days I would answer her: Not so, Mama: things are evidence; life accumulates on them, like the snow that falls while you're sleeping.

I glance across the room at my old couch and remember when I first saw it, in the early 1980s. It was at the

Jewish Women Council Thrift Shop; the shop has since moved, or closed, but it was then located on the corner of Ninth Avenue and 54th Street. The couch was shabby and soiled, but it was shapely, and just the right size. I paid fifty dollars for it, paid a lot more to have it reupholstered, and we placed it under the south windows of our living room on Riverside Drive. In the afternoons when it was washed in light from the river it was my favorite place to lie down and read. And for thirty years everyone who came to visit us sat on it. I like to think that the cushions still hold imprints of the bottoms of our old friends; and of our now-absent friends, and of these last, *how* their numbers mount as the years go by. That couch was the seat of our married life.

Your watch, for another example, which is now my watch by default. You wore it every day. On a recent morning I buckled it on my wrist and noticed how worn the leather strap had become, and I thought about what sort of new strap you might approve of. I thought about your tastes in furniture and clothes, and wondered if you would like the apartment where I now live with our couch, and your watch, and a few of our other things. Thoughts came to me about our life together, and about the day in the hospital I knew would be our last, when the nurse kindly suggested that I take the watch from your wrist and the wedding ring from your finger.

Not long ago I stopped to look at an amethyst bracelet in a jeweler's window, which made me think of the amethyst pin I once gave my mother: an etched gold bar with the purple stone prettily set in the center. I remembered where I bought it for her, in an antiques shop on MacDougal Street, in the days when there were such shops on that street. Then I thought about the ways in which MacDougal Street has changed, and how so many of the shops and cafés I once knew are gone, how much the city has changed, and how the solid landmarks of your life vanish and you can't even remember what they were: I pass a building that wasn't there the last time I passed, but what building *was* there? And my mother's pin. Where *is* it? Whose thieving hand took it from her drawer? Whenever I think of that pin I am struck with the sharp pain of its absence.

I have other things that belonged to my mother— heirlooms I suppose, if a jewel becomes an heirloom in only one generation. I have the silver flower pin that her friend Tillie gave her, one of those swirling Georg Jensen designs that was fashionable in the 1950s; I have the battered silver compact I once bought for her because it was engraved with an ornate *B*, which happened to be her initial. Also, in my living room, I have the porch chair that my father rocked himself on, green-painted wooden slats bolted to a springy, iron frame. The iron has worn to black, the layers of paint are flaking; these days people congratulate me on finding such an excellent example of shabby chic. I think how scornfully amused my father would be to learn that the chair he bought at a hardware store named Green's for five dollars—actually he bought a pair of them for that price—has morphed into an expensive home-decorating item. "Ha!" he would say. "How much?"

Sometimes, from piety, I wear my mother's silver flower pin, sometimes I look at myself in the clouded mirror of her compact, sometimes I rock myself in my father's chair, almost every day I wear your watch, except for dressy occasions when I wear my mother's watch.

Nominally, it was my mother's watch. I never actually saw her wear it. She thought it was too good to wear, and I almost think so too. It's a beautiful thing, more bracelet than watch, the most precious piece of jewelry my mother ever owned, delicately wrought in 18-karat rose gold, with a narrow open-work gold band, a cunning catch engraved with her initials, and a face so tiny you have to squint to read the time. It was made to show off the narrow wrist of a lady who wore rings on her fingers and diamonds in her ears and could be careless of time. Not my mother's style, which was plain to the point of stylelessness, and I must add that her wrist was a little too broad for that narrow band.

My father's sister, Leah, brought the watch to my mother as a gift in honor of their first meeting. Of course she did not then know what sort of watch my mother would have liked, or what sort of woman her brother had married; in fact, she barely remembered her brother, whom she had not seen since she was seven years old, when he was a bit more than twice her age. By the time Leah turned up in our lives they had been lost to each other for more than forty years.

Before we learned of Leah's existence, it had never occurred to me that my father might have a family. By the time I was born I think he had forgotten about them, or assumed they were all dead. In any case, he never spoke of parents or sisters or brothers. He was, by nature, a silent man; he never gave me much to go on, and I had never imagined him young, nor did I even know the name of the town where he had been born. "A hard man," I heard Leah say to my mother's sister, Frieda. "Just like his father." So now I knew something. And in the few weeks of Leah's first visit she drew for me the indelible picture of an angry, restless boy living in a place called Lomazy, a dismal small town in Russian Poland ("There was nothing there, *nothing*"), at unreconcilable odds with his father; a boy with only two prospects before him—the tannery, which his father owned, or the rabbinate—prospects he could not stomach. Without a word, he ran away, leaving his parents, a brother, and three sisters. His parents knew only that this wayward son had stowed away on a ship to America; they knew that much only because the stowaway had been caught. My grandfather was persuaded to send the money for his passage, and eventually my father repaid him. The envelope from America that reached Lomazy in, perhaps, 1914 was postmarked Galveston, Texas. There was only a money order inside: "No note," Leah said. "Not even, 'Don't worry about me, I'm fine.'" The family never heard from him again.

By then the First World War had broken out, the Russian Revolution followed, then the Polish-Soviet war. The family survived, although my father did not know it; as far as Leah knew, he had made no inquiries. In the mid-1920s, Leah married. She and her husband emigrated to Argentina. They settled in Buenos Aires. Leah was a good daughter and kept in touch with her family in Poland. All through the 1930s cards and letters were exchanged. In 1939 silence fell. By the time the war ended, Leah knew that every Jew in Lomazy had been murdered.

After that, more and more often, she thought of her brother, somewhere on the vast continent of America. When war refugees from Poland came through Buenos Aires, shuffled from one country to another, to America, if they could get in, or to Israel, to Canada, she asked each traveler if he had heard of her brother. The answer was always no. Then, in the early 1950s, a distant cousin from Israel turned up at her door. He was on his way to New York. "Look for my brother," Leah said, and a year or two later my father, mother, and I were on the dock when Leah's ship sailed into New York harbor. Among the hundreds of disembarking passengers we recognized a woman wearing my father's face. She came directly toward us as though she were looking in a mirror, bearing my mother's golden watch and my father's story. Both now belong to me, the story inseparable from the watch as though it had been packed in like a warranty.

So many things, so much to think about. Like the early summer morning, many years ago, when I happened to be walking down a street on the Upper East Side, one of those surprisingly intact nineteenth-century streets of elegant townhouses. It was so early that the trash was just being put out for collection. Something sailed up from a basement areaway and fell at my feet. It was a piece of heavy fabric, the color of dried clay. I picked it up; it was a substantial piece of material, about three by four feet, roughly loomed, handloomed it seemed to me, and when I unfolded it I saw that it was decorated with beads. Bands of rust-colored and yellow beads, each color block artfully separated by a small design of black and white beads. Some beads were missing, and in the spaces I could see the pencil lines that had been drawn to guide the sewer's hand; the edges of the canvaslike material were shredded and irregular, and I suppose those damages caused it to be thrown away. Given away, to me, to whom the imperfections of this artifact were further adornments. I took the piece home and put it on the back of a chair, where it has remained, on the back of one chair or another, in one apartment or another. At first the pleasure it gave me was for itself alone, and for my luck in finding it. But now, as the years have passed, it is so immeasurably enriched by thoughts of that summer morning when I was young, fresh from the bed of a new lover, walking with the rising sun down an unfamiliar street, suddenly delighted by the piece of fabric that had fallen at my feet; a time when I was without a clue as to what lay ahead of me in the life that I now look back on, still innocent of all the things that would come my way.

Ballerina

IN A LONG-AGO SPRING, just as daffodils began to sprout, I began a new love affair. By the time the leaves crackled underfoot it was over. Six months, then, for the *actual* relationship, which was about average for me in those days. But it was my practice to follow a broken love affair with several months of anguished tears rounded off by anger; in this way I could get almost a year out of it. Foolish girl, you say; she thinks she has all the time in the world.

In this particular case, when my tears had dried, and I cast about for material to fuel anger, the only thing I could come up with was: *That bastard! He thinks he's such hot shit, showing off with his cameras and his light meters and his fancy darkroom.* That wouldn't do, I knew better. He *was* a good photographer, and he *did* produce gorgeous black-and-white prints in his well-equipped darkroom. In happier days, he'd given me one of his photographs: a picture of lumber. It doesn't sound like much, but I promise you it's something: a still life of large planks of rough wood, varying in length and width, stacked haphazardly in the doorway of a barn. The photographer had seen the art in the accidental arrangement, in the deeply grained beauty of the wood, in the way the light hit the stack; he had framed the subject perfectly, and printed the image in rich tones, ranging from the velvet black of the barn's interior, to the warmest grays and browns of the wood, to the brightness of sunlight where it struck. Whenever I looked at the picture it made me envious; it made me wish to be a photographer myself. A wish without hope, I thought; as hopeless as my wish to be a ballerina whenever I went to the ballet.

But, as it happened, one night that winter I was at a party where a stranger offered to sell me a 35mm Minolta, plus two extra lenses, for forty dollars. At any other moment in my life, I would have said no.

Not long after that, I made a drastic change in my life. I quit my job as a magazine editor, moved out of my

Upper West Side apartment, and for most of the 1970s I lived in a Bowery loft, and earned my living as a freelance writer. In the mornings I worked at my typewriter; in the afternoons, I took my Minolta out for a walk. It occurs to me now that walking with a camera is not unlike walking a dog. A dog walker is really an appendage of the dog, walks at the pace the dog sets, stops when the dog stops, sees what the dog sees—other dogs and their walkers, stray cats, disgusting items on the ground that smell interesting to a dog. When I walked with my camera, I paid attention to what would interest a camera; it was my license to loiter and look. I walked the streets slowly, like a hunter or a prowler, alert to light and shadow, to discarded items, to people in groups, to solitary figures, to buildings and alleys, always in wait for the moment when a picture might show itself to me.

In the first year or so, I took a lot of bad pictures. But I wasn't discouraged, I was hooked, and spurred to educate myself. There weren't many galleries devoted to photographs in those days, but I became a regular at the few that existed. I paged though books of photographs and bought quite a lot of them, I collected hundreds of photographs on postcards. The images that stirred me were the black-and-white classics of early to mid-twentieth-century photography—Paul Strand, Walker Evans, Dorothea Lange, André Kertész, Helen Levitt, Cartier-Bresson. I signed up for workshops with some good photographers, and I took a workshop with Lisette Model, a great one. My pictures got better. Lisette Model, herself, told me so. She uttered the magic words: "You have an eye," she said. She also said that if I was serious, seeing and snapping the shutter wasn't enough; it was necessary to understand and control the entire process, from negative to print.

That was discouraging. I had no conviction that I could master anything technical. And anyway, how could I set up a darkroom in a loft with no real bathroom or enclosed kitchen? Then, one day, on Prince Street, only a few blocks west of my loft, I saw a small sign over a basement areaway: RICHARD BORST / DARKROOMS FOR RENT. If he has been forgotten, let me praise his name. I thought he was an old guy, but he was probably only in his late fifties then, always in need of a shave and a bath. He supplemented his income as a photographer by setting up darkrooms, four or five of them, in his basement studio. Three dollars an hour, chemicals and advice included. Richard Borst taught me the basics of darkroom technique, he was always available to answer questions, offer suggestions, praise a print, or damn it. He never mentioned that in his basement studio I would learn a deep secret of happiness.

Each time I closed the door of the darkroom behind me, and my eyes adjusted to the dim amber safelight, all the distracting, niggling anxieties of daily life fell away. I entered a state of effortless concentration, of complete absorption in the work of developing film, exposing the negatives, immersing them in their various chemical baths. Writing was hard, grinding work; in the darkroom, every decision about making a print came without struggle. I saw immediately what had to be done—this tone deepened, another lightened, this area cropped out, that one enlarged. I just *knew*. Hours disappeared, afternoon turned into night, and when I finally opened the door to leave, I felt euphoric and calm, as if I'd been on a great drug high.

I took some good pictures in those years, and I made some good prints. To this day I'm amazed that they're mine. But at the end of the seventies, when rising rents in Soho forced Richard to closed the darkroom, I wasn't entirely distressed. I had begun to feel that I had reached the end of my picture-taking life. My photographs varied in subjects and locations—a man walking in heavy rain, bent beneath his umbrella; a lone black crow flying across a great, ancient chalk horse carved into an English hillside; huge black rocks marching out to sea on a deserted Oregon beach, a landing place for the birds flying in; empty restaurant tables, taken through a plate glass window; a rag mop lit by the rising sun, hanging from the dirty window of a Bowery flophouse. I saw that these images were studies in loneliness, they were autobiography and I'd come to the end of the story. Without deciding to, I walked my camera less and less.

A few days after Christmas in 1980, I went uptown to return a sweater to Bloomingdale's. It was a mild, windless winter day. The sky an overcast pearl gray, the air moist and fresh with the promise of snow. I walked aimlessly, window-shopping my way up Lexington Avenue. On a side street I noticed a row of black limousines parked outside a church. Wedding? Funeral? I stopped.

In a minute or two, a bride and groom in full wedding regalia, stepped out the church door. At that moment, as if waiting for the occasion, large snowflakes began to hover in the air. The bridal couple made their way slowly down the church steps, in time to the white tribute falling as slowly as the notes of a processional. A sudden breeze blew up; the bride's veil floated into the pearl-gray sky, forming a net for the snowflakes. I caught my breath at the beauty of it—the stylized figures, the brilliance of the white gown, the black of the tuxedo, the floating veil, all enveloped in the luminous gray light. I didn't have my camera but I still had the habit: my eye framed the photograph that might have been. I was filled with regret.

I don't remember how I spent the New Year's Eve of 1980, but in early January, we met for dinner at a Greek restaurant. It was our second date, but the first time we were alone. You had a discussion with the waiter about ordering our meal. In Greek. I couldn't top that. But I told you various things about myself: about the book I was working on, about living on the Bowery, about taking pictures, and I told you about my recently lost picture of the bride and groom.

You were quite taken, I could see that, even after I mentioned my taste for country-western music. You thought I had an interesting, if solitary life. You thought I was in need of rescue. And only two weeks later you confessed that it had occurred to you in the restaurant, when scarcely half an hour had passed since I'd taken off my coat, while my first glass of wine was still half full, that the wedding scene was an omen for us.

Royal We

THERE WAS NO TYPEWRITER in our house when I was growing up. Anyone who needed to write something down took up pencil or pen. Most often that person was my mother. Almost every afternoon she sat at the kitchen table writing a letter of family news to one or another of her many friends and relatives. She used a fountain pen with blue ink, and in her neat, loopy cursive, she thriftily covered both sides of plain white notepaper. After I left home, she wrote to me. Her handwriting is as familiar to me as her face; I'd know it in my dreams, as I do, when I dream that a letter from her has come in the mail. I never seem to read the letter; the sight of my name on the envelope, written in her hand, is enough.

My own handwriting was always execrable. This distressed my mother. She, an immigrant, for whom

English was a third language, one which she had struggled to master, had a daughter who had been born to the language, and yet formed its alphabet so carelessly. For several of my childhood summers she made me spend an hour a day practicing my handwriting, to little effect and with many quarrels. Eventually she gave up on this project. When I graduated from high school she bought me a typewriter and insisted that I take a typing course.

That typewriter was an Olivetti Lettera, a portable, very popular in the 1950s. It is now enshrined in the Museum of Modern Art as an icon of modernist design. I never liked it much. It was more toy than tool, so flimsy that it jumped every time I struck a key. In the early 1970s, when my mother decided to take typing lessons herself, I gave the Olivetti back to her and went shopping for a replacement.

In those days I knew a guy named Fred. Everybody knew a Fred; he was the guy who knew all the places in the city where anything a person wanted could be bought for practically nothing. Fred took me down to Centre Street, to a two-story warehouse jumbled with old office furniture—partners' desks, rolltop desks, wooden swivel armchairs, and dozens and dozens of manual office typewriters orphaned by the advent of the electric typewriter.

It didn't take long for me to spot the one I wanted. Among the heaps of 1950s-vintage office typewriters, I saw something glamorous. I recognized it from old movies: from *His Girl Friday* (1940), for instance, where the reporter, a cigarette dangling from his lips, types his copy with one finger while shouting into the candlestick-shaped telephone of the era.

This typewriter had been manufactured in the mid-1930s. In its day it was ordinary, no one had *ooohed* and *aaahed* over it. But time had magicked it; like some old cars and farm tools, it had matured into beauty. Made of black-enameled steel, it stood tall and proud, shoulders wide, ivory-colored keys bezel-set in steel rims, enamel-encased ribbon spools not hidden, but sitting below the carriage like perfect little breasts. Rectangular glass panels on either side of the machine showed off its inner workings, and ornate gilt lettering identified the maker: Royal in name, royal in elegance. It weighed a ton. Only a porter could have made it portable.

I tried it out: it took a bit of energy to push the keys down, more to return the carriage. I liked the effort; it felt like the overture to work. And hard as I pounded on it, the machine maintained its dignified immobility. Twenty dollars changed hands; and another twenty for a desk with a cutout typewriter well, into which the Royal fit perfectly.

At the time my mother gave me the Olivetti, her ambitions for me were modest. She no longer had any hopes of attending my graduation from law school, or even from a teacher's college. She hoped only that her boy-and-clothes-crazed daughter would be equipped with at least one skill to sell on the job market. And once I had learned to touch-type, so it proved to be. At first I worked in typing pools, then as a clerk-typist, then as a secretary. I changed jobs often. After a while I got a job at a magazine, writing captions for pictures; pretty soon, I was writing the stories that went with them. And before Mama and I could get over our astonishment, I was earning a living by writing things. With a byline.

Of course I could have called myself a writer. But we were readers, my mother and I, we had our standards: Tolstoy, Dostoyevsky, Dickens, George Eliot—*they* were writers. What did that make me?

37

"What is the kid doing now?" my mother's friends would ask.

"Oh," said my mother, "she's doing some work for a magazine."

I wouldn't say that I had anything so precise as a plan when I quit my job at the magazine. I was still young, I believed that everything was possible. At this point I thought that if I kept my expenses low, I could make a living freelancing articles for magazines. And given enough time, I might turn myself into the kind of writer that my mother and I could credit. In any case, I knew that I could always get another job at another magazine. We were, after all, living in the golden age of print; magazines and literary journals spilled from the racks at every newsstand in town.

I moved from my relatively expensive apartment on the Upper West Side to a many-windowed loft on the Bowery. I placed my desk against a narrow slice of wall between two tall south-facing windows, put a red pillow on a wheeled, adjustable-height wooden piano stool, and started typing. Over the next decade, I typed many hundreds of thousands of words on the Royal, most of them headed for the trash, but also dozens of articles that paid the rent; and then, many drafts of my first book.

From the distance of the computer, I can see that the typewriter is the barest intervention between hand and paper. Like handiwork, it forgives no mistakes. In a clean copy a dropped line can mean retyping an entire day's work, just as a dropped stitch in knitting may require unraveling half a sweater. The typist who changes her mind about where a paragraph should be placed needs scissors and Scotch tape to move the section around; the number of drafts needed to achieve a clean copy are endless; as for making copies of the finished work, carbon paper and onionskin was the only option. It was work to work on a typewriter, but, as far as typewriters go, I lucked out with the Royal. Never once did it break down, never once did it give me the slightest trouble. And it needed so little in the way of maintenance—regular dusting, fresh ribbons, clotted ink cleaned from the letter keys once in a while, a dust cover for its nighttime hours.

Sometimes, now, when I'm going through my files,

I come across a fragile, browning page that was typed on the Royal. I can see the typewriter's idiosyncrasies and my own: the Royal's broken-tail "q," its out-of-alignment capital letters, the red band of the ribbon showing a little of itself at the edges of the black type, the way it reproduced the differing pressure of my fingers; and then I notice how overgenerous I am with the comma, my habitual misspellings (*mispellings*), the use of "gentiles" for "genitals" (how often could *that* have happened?). These habits of mine, and the Royal's, are as distinguishing as handwriting. As Alger Hiss learned to his regret. As any forensic typewriter analyst would testify, should I ever be sued for plagerism. I mean *plagiarism*.

"What do you do?" you asked me when we met.

"Oh. I'm doing some research for a book about this anarchist."

"So you're a professional researcher?"

"Well, no. Actually, I'm doing research for my own book."

You were quite severe: "You're writing a book? Well, then, *say* you're a writer."

Not many months later I packed up the Royal, my

clothes, some pieces of furniture, and moved uptown to live with you for the next thirty years. That was long enough to put the Royal in the closet and learn to use a computer. Long enough for your daughters to grow up and have their own sons and daughters. Long enough for me to watch as you grew as gaunt as Christ on the cross, to hear the struggle of your breath, for you to become tired, *bone*-tired with the hard work it took just to stay alive. Long enough for me to wake up every morning and wonder: Is *this* the day? I came across a line in an Alice Munro story: *Yes, it's time; there has to be something, here it is.* There it was, a few months after the party we gave to celebrate your seventy-third birthday.

I wanted to move downtown again. I was consumed by the idea that if I went back to my old loft, picked up where I had left off, history might repeat itself. I'm told that the bereft are often visited by such notions. In any case, the real estate moguls had gotten downtown ahead of me. I couldn't afford to live on the Bowery, now pricier, and certainly trendier, than Park Avenue.

So I'm still in the neighborhood. When I walk over to Broadway to buy fish at Citarella's, or coffee at Zabar's,

I pass the corner of 77th Street. I always look west for a glimpse of our bedroom and bathroom windows. I want you to know that I still have our couch, a few small tables, and a couple of chairs. Remember that ancient little oak chest—the one with the date, "1673," carved on the front? It's sitting at the foot of a bookcase, just behind the desk where I work on my computer. Should you lift the lid, you'd see a small thermos bottle, which is doing double duty as your urn. Above the chest, four shelves up, is the Royal, another relic that doesn't do useful work anymore.

I like the computer, but after all these years, I still haven't a clue as to how the letters I click on the keyboard make their way to the screen; I still get pleasure from its "cut" and "paste" functions, by the way it absorbs inserted words and paragraphs without blinking. And I'm in constant fear of the one wrong click that will make everything disappear.

I'll never go back to the typewriter. But if an amputee still feels the missing limb, I still hear the clack of typewriter keys, the *ching* of the bell at the end of a line, feel the satisfying strike of my fingers on the keys, the reach of my arm to return the carriage—all second nature to me in that evanescent decade when I typed away, sometimes glancing through the window at the downtown sweep of the Bowery, aware of the light as it changed from morning to afternoon, from season to season, until you came along.

All those years ago, you said I was a writer. I decided to believe you. Ever after, you were my first reader. I waited on your opinion. I wait now.

Chicken Pox

CHICKEN POX. My doctor asked me if I'd ever had it. I wasn't sure. I had a flickering memory of being carried into a darkened room, put to bed, and ordered not to scratch. But that could have been German measles, or even a bad case of poison ivy.

Who would know?

Of course my mother would have known. Her three sisters would have known too. My aunts knew everything my mother knew about me, and they were not shy about expressing their opinions. When my aunt Frieda called me a spoiled brat, she was speaking for four. But it's been a long time since those women, the women of my life, have been available to chide me, or answer questions.

*

My mother was close to eighty by the time you met her. So what did you think? She was very quiet, shy of you, nervous that she might say or do anything to embarrass me. She was still a pretty woman, wasn't she? Deeply wrinkled from all those years of worshipping the sun, but her lips were still full, her eyes hazel green, she wore her salt-and-pepper hair in an immigrant's long braid that she twisted into a bun. And she was tiny, probably two inches down from her youthful height of 5'2". In your honor she'd worn a white blouse and black skirt, the most presentable items in her scanty wardrobe.

She gave you no hint of how clever she was, that she'd had a gift for gaiety, had loved to tell stories, had earnestly improved herself with night classes, had been queen bee of her large family—those three sisters, plus three brothers, plus their husbands, wives, and children, and one rebellious daughter, to say nothing of my father, who was no piece of cake. Just imagine the arguments and quarrels, the hurt feelings, the ancient grievances she'd had to soothe and negotiate to keep that unit intact. Once upon a time her plate was full.

Then, one by one, we all left her. It was as if we'd been living at a railroad station waiting for our trains to come in. One by one we boarded, and left her standing alone on the platform, waving goodbye, growing smaller and smaller until the train rounded a bend.

I didn't go very far, but it was to a life that mostly excluded her. Frieda, her best-loved sister, was soon killed by a runaway car. Georgie, her youngest brother, died young. The others dispersed to warmer climates, and after a while her telephone seldom rang, almost no one came to visit. And now, when I count up the years, I see that she has been dead for more than a quarter of a century. That's a dignified slice of time, a strong indication that she'll remain in that state, no matter how often I call for her. You, on the other hand, are less than eight years old in death, a child, unreliable. For all I know, you might yet decide to turn up.

The arithmetic seems to matter. Sometimes these mornings, as I'm waking up, I hear myself say: *Mama.* That's only fair, isn't it? I've been without her so much longer than I've been without you. And let me point out that I wasn't your first wife, but I was always her one and only. "Mama" was the first word I ever said, and if she is an example, it may be my last. Remember that day I went to see her in the nursing home? It was a couple of weeks before she died; for the first time in our lives

46

she looked at me without recognition. She said to *me*: "Have you seen my mother?"

Every year, from the time I was a babe in arms until I was almost grown, my mother and I spent our summers upstate, in the house my father had built. During those months, two of my aunts, and sometimes all three at once, came to stay with us, and until the husbands arrived on weekends I lived in a house of women, in a bath of their constant conversation.

One hot afternoon I was alone in my room, lost in the world of a Ray Bradbury story. My aunt Frieda's voice distracted me. She was walking up the pathway, talking to her friend Rose. I hoped they'd keep moving along to the kitchen but they settled on the porch just outside my open window, and Frieda said: "But Rose, you know that before Bella had the kid, she had a lot of trouble with her pregnancies."

I stopped reading.

Bella was my mother.

I was the kid.

Pregnan*cies*?

"Yes," Frieda said, "two miscarriages."

I was ten years old. I knew what a miscarriage was. Our neighbor, Sophie, had had one, and I'd paid close attention to the murmurs of commiseration when she brought the news to my mother and my aunts. Sophie had been three months along.

But *my* mother?

This was too disturbing to think about. I went back to my story about time travel.

But that night when I was in bed, how I tossed and turned! My little brain teemed with existential questions. Well, I say existential, as if I knew what it meant. Let's just say I was worried about the problem of my existence.

What if my mother had given birth to a child before I was born? Would that child have been *me*? What if it had been someone else? Would I have been born later, with an older sister or brother in my place? Would I not have been my mother's precious only? Or—banish the thought!—would I never have been born at all? What if I had been one of my mother's miscarriages? Or! What if my mother and father had never met? If their parents had never met? I would never even have been as close to life as a miscarriage. Never a me? Not even in embryo? *Inconceivable!* And no one would know that I hadn't been born; even I wouldn't know; there wouldn't have been an I. Neither would my mother know that it was *me* she had lost! Oh, my poor mama! To live her life with strangers for children!

On that summer night the door to the universe cracked open to give me a glimpse of a world as strange and terrifying as the science fiction I had been reading. A world made by randomness, by contingency, by chance, by luck. *Nothing* was meant to be. In that moment I knew it was true. It was unbearable. *No.* I turned away.

Look! Here I was! I *had* been born. I was in *my* house, in *my* bed. My mother was asleep upstairs. If I called out for her now, she'd come running. When I got up in the morning she'd make me breakfast. In the evening she'd cook dinner. If I'd *had* chicken pox she'd have stayed up with me all night. She and her sisters would go on talking and talking, she'd go on loving me, she'd be my mother forever. Nothing would change.

The Goods

I WASN'T VERY EDUCABLE. That was sad for you, given your habit of mentoring young women along literature's path. "Meet my wife," you'd say, "she's set in her ways."

It was true that I hadn't read Adorno, Gramsci, or Lukács; I tried *Ulysses* and tried again, never making it more than halfway through; I certainly didn't go on to *Finnegans Wake*. Okay, I would read Proust, but I wouldn't be rushed. Classical music put me to sleep. I more or less refused poetry unless it was sung by Bob Dylan or Leonard Cohen or John Prine. Also, I didn't care much for the theater, which you loved second only to the books I hadn't read. How would I hold your interest?

Like Scheherazade, I entertained you with stories beyond your ken. I could narrate the villainous lives of

Lucky Luciano, Vito Genovese, and Carmine Galante; I knew many interesting details about Stalinist machinations during the Spanish Civil War; about Mussolini's pre-Fascist life as a Socialist, and his friendship with Angelica Balabanov; about the early Wobbly strikes in Massachusetts and New Jersey. I knew something, although not nearly enough, about the maddeningly esoteric arguments among various Italian-American anarchist factions in the early part of the twentieth century. Also, I had information about a mysterious man named Enea Sormenti, aka Vittorio Vidali and Comandante Carlos, who was suspiciously nearby when Trotsky was assassinated.

I had plans for these stories. When I had finished sorting them out they would blend seamlessly into a larger story and appear in print between two covers. That day was more distant than I could have imagined, and I did not yet know of all the impediments that would spring up along my way. I was still lighthearted when we met.

So. I was writing this biography about someone named Carlo Tresca. You'd never heard of him. *I'd* never heard of him until one evening, when I was at a dinner party, someone mentioned his name in my hearing. I eaves-dropped. It seemed that this person was an Italian immi-grant, an anarchist, and he'd been mysteriously murdered on Fifth Avenue. I liked a good murder story, but I knew almost nothing about anarchists, I didn't know the Ital-ian language, and I had never tried my hand at extensive research. Nevertheless, and much to my surprise, when I woke up the morning after I'd heard Tresca's name for the first time, I discovered that I had made a decision to write his life. Was it a whim? I like to think it was recognition.

Actually, I wasn't all that lighthearted. If you wanted to hear my stories, you had to listen to my anxieties. I was obsessed about the safety of my research notes and doc-uments. The more I stuffed my file cabinets with papers, the more I worried that they would somehow disappear. A thief in the night? Fire, more likely. Remember that night I woke you up in a panic? I'd heard a siren go by, and I *knew*, I just *knew*, that a fire had broken out in the ratty building where I had my office; all my precious work was going up in flames. You laughed at this par-ticular terror, and then pointed out the availability of fireproof file cabinets. That worked. But what could you do when I learned that I had a competitor, Nunzio Pernicone. What could *anybody* do about Nunzio the Messenger, so euphoniously and aptly named? Sometime in the future—maybe tomorrow, maybe in a year—he would publish *his* biography of Tresca. Nunzio's voice whispered in my ear: *You think you know so much. Ha! You don't know* anything. *I'm the one who* really *knows. And you* know *I know!*

Oh, yes, I knew. In complete ignorance I had decided to write about this obscure Italian-American who'd been dead for forty years. Ignorance had given me confidence, made me blithe, allowed me to feel that I could actually write such a book. In my ignorance I believed that *I* had discovered the territory and planted my flag. As far as I knew, no one else had any interest in this Tresca person, except for a few very elderly anarchists whom I planned to interview. So imagine my distress when, a year or so into my project, I learned that I was a squatter in the house that Nunzio owned; my sources belonged to him.

"Are you Nunzio's assistant?" the elderly anarchists asked me when I turned up at the door. "Oh, he's so handsome," the female anarchists added. Nunzio had been hard at work on Tresca for many years. And he was a *professor*, a PhD, an acknowledged authority on my subject. His father had *known* Carlo Tresca. Baby Nunzio had probably been dandled on Tresca's knee! Who had more right to the subject: the dilettante or the scholar?

In those Googleless days it took some digging to track Nunzio down, but I finally found him, teaching at a university in Illinois. What did I think would be gained by calling him up? Ignorance, and innocence in the ways of scholarly rivalry, allowed me to hope that he might welcome me as a colleague, be interested in what I had to say; we would talk shop, exchange information.

Oh, no. He was incredulous when I called, *really* pissed off. Finally he said:

"You're fluent in Italian, I suppose."

"*Dov'è il bagno per favore?*" I said. "*Prego.*"

He laughed. "Go right ahead with whatever it is you're doing. My book is almost finished."

I put down the phone. I was sitting at my desk in my ratty office, surrounded by my new fireproof file cabinets. I'd never felt so demoralized. His book was almost finished. What was the point of going on? I thought about the time I had invested, about how hard I'd

"To Daffodils"
BY <u>ROBERT HERRICK</u>

Fair Daffodils, we weep to see
You haste away so soon;
As yet the early-rising sun
Has not attain'd his noon.
Stay, stay,
Until the hasting day
Has run
But to the even-song;
And, having pray'd together, we
Will go with you along.

We have short time to stay, as you,
We have as short a spring;
As quick a growth to meet decay,
As you, or anything.
We die
As your hours do, and dry
Away,
Like to the summer's rain;
Or as the pearls of morning's dew,
Ne'er to be found again.

worked to gather my material, about how much work was still ahead of me, about how much worse I'd feel if I gave up now. I thought about the future. I thought about the rave reviews Nunzio's book would receive. I thought about the review my book would get, if I was lucky enough to get any notice at all. To take the curse off, I decided to write the review myself:

After almost forty years of silence, we seem to be in the midst of a Carlo Tresca revival, if these two recently published books are any indication. The first of these, by Professor Nunzio Pernicone, is meticulously researched and lucidly written. Professor Pernicone's deep understanding of his subject and his sure grasp of historical fact place Carlo Tresca firmly in his time, and so illuminate a period long obscured by doctrinal confusion.

And then there is the bizarre volume by Dorothy Gallagher. Ms. Gallagher is not a historian, and her freedom from academic strictures has led her to some interesting conjectures. Her belief, for example, that Tresca was not Italian, but Romanian, seems inexplicable, as does her insistence that World War II preceded World War I. However, we may be dealing here with an original mind, and it has occurred to this reviewer that these apparently gross errors, which seem to bear no relation to historical fact, are in fact deliberate. A reader who does not immediately dismiss this book as the work of a moron may be rewarded by perceiving an underlying pattern in Tresca's life and death laid bare by an artfully—nay, brilliantly—conceived pattern of what a more conventional mind might consider to be ludicrous errors.

A couple of years after we spoke on the phone, Nunzio came to New York. I went to the conference where he was presenting a paper on Tresca. I noticed that he was tall and very handsome, I noticed that he spoke Italian as fluently as English. I noticed that he *really*, but *really* knew his stuff. I introduced myself.

"Oh," he said in greeting. "My book is almost finished."

But, since he realized that he hadn't scared me off, we talked a little, we had coffee, and we became, if not exactly friends, warily friendly. We met whenever he came to town, we had lunch, we talked shop. As colleagues, as equals, or so I preferred to think. I invited him home to meet you.

Years passed. Nunzio's book didn't appear. Finally, in 1988, my book was published. It did get reviews. The reviews were good. How happy we were.

I sent Nunzio a copy. He didn't comment directly, but he asked if he could borrow some of my research materials. That made me proud.

I was amazed that I had been first out of the gate. And many years passed before Nunzio published his book. He sent me a copy. I was afraid to read it. I knew how good it was. I turned to the title page and read his inscription:

For Dorothy,
   I know better than anyone that your biography of Tresca was a tough act to follow. I hope you consider my effort to have met the task.

Until that moment I thought I'd pulled a fast one. I'd been waiting for Nunzio's approbation. At last I felt legitimate.

Nunzio and I lost touch. I missed my colleague, my rival. Just knowing he was there had kept me on my mettle, given me a standard. I thought about him from time to time, and one day, not long ago, I went to Google to see what he was up to. I wanted to send him a note. His obituary was dated only a few days earlier.

Now, listen to me. I don't know where you are, or who you're hanging out with. Probably you're having drinks with Alex and Edward, and some pretty girls who, luckily for you, had died young. But tear yourself away. I want you to ask directions to the section where they keep the anarchists. You'll hear them before you see them, still loudly haranguing each other about their various versions of utopia. Trying to untangle the details of those arguments used to drive me crazy. These people were Nunzio's life; if you don't see him right away he'll be nearby. He's the tall handsome one. And when you do see him, I want you to give him a message. Tell him how much he meant to me. Tell him I always knew that he was the one with the goods.

Pigeon Season

MIKE TYSON SAID that if you make friends with a pigeon you'll never be lonely. I read that somewhere. Elsewhere I've read that the pigeon is host to lice and various diseases dangerous to humans. From personal experience I know that pigeons shit—make guano, if you prefer—on everything. A low-flying pigeon once made guano on top of my head: I felt a warm plop, as if someone had broken an egg, and a moment later greenish slime dripped down my glasses. *Ugh!*

In fairness to the pigeon, I acknowledge that I've always liked seeing them in certain of their aspects. I like to see a flock in flight, dipping, rising, gleaming, darkening, turning and swirling like a corps de ballet. And when I find myself walking toward home on 100th Street in the early evening, I always stop to check out the six-story building at the corner of Manhattan Avenue, which is where the local flock gathers at twilight. Dozens and dozens of pigeons, maybe a hundred or more of them, line up along the roof of the tenement, arraying themselves like toy sentries, standing perfectly still, wing to wing, the shape of each plump breast and small round head outlined in the last light. For a moment I feel transported to an ancient city, so much do they resemble a sculpted frieze crowning a Roman ruin.

But when two pigeons landed on my terrace at the beginning of last July, I was not pleased. I clapped my hands, stamped my feet, and cried *Shoo!* Jenny happened to be visiting that day. "This is *completely* unacceptable!" she told them, a phrase that would have been familiar to her students. The insolent creatures didn't even pretend to flutter their wings; they just shuffled around the corner where, for several minutes, I heard them making their guttural coos. Soon they took wing. Good riddance, so I thought. A week later, when I was watering the plants, I saw a gleam in the dirt: two small white eggs almost hidden under the shrubs in one of the planters. Ah! *That's* what they'd been up to! I called Jenny. If she hadn't been so appalled, I'd have thrown the eggs off the side of the building.

*

Did I tell you that Jenny has left town? Yes, Jenny, the first friend I introduced to you in our courtship days. The Jenny about whom you said: "pure as spring water." So about a year ago, without a by-your-leave, she announced that she and Joel were moving upstate. I *know* that the city has become too expensive, I *know* that paying rent on an apartment, *plus* on Jenny's studio, was a strain. But what about *me*? What about our forty-four-year friendship? What is distance if not distancing? So many of our friends have followed your example, or otherwise drifted out of my life (our old friend Ed, for one, trailing a list of grievances) that I'm down to bare bones in the old-friends department. As was my mother when she grew old.

"Mama," I once asked her, "where's Rose? Why doesn't she come to see you anymore?"

"It just goes to show, darling," she said.

Was that cryptic wisdom, or dementia?

The moment I decided not to throw the pigeon eggs off the roof, I became attached to them. They were so

61

small, so perfectly egg-shaped, so *purposeful*. And they had been laid virtually at my doorstep. I'd been entrusted. But why had they been left exposed to my sight? To the sight of any passing predator? Had their parents abandoned them? No. There was a pigeon almost hidden in the bushes, just outside the iron railing. As soon as I stepped away from the nest he squeezed through the bars and settled himself on the eggs. It *was* a he, as I learned—the father.

Do you know that pigeons rate near the top of the bird intelligence scale? Maybe ravens and parrots are smarter, but pigeons recognize individual human faces and voices; they recognize themselves in a mirror; they can be trained to carry messages. During World War Two, a pigeon sent out by a farmer in the Netherlands reached British lines with a message taped to its leg: "Help our Jews." Even if you blindfold pigeons and transport them thousands of miles away from their homes, by some still-mysterious method they find their way back.

Moreover, pigeons are a species of doves. Nobody despises the dove, nobody refers to doves as "flying rats." Noah sent a dove to bring back a sign that the waters were receding. The ancient Egyptians prized doves for their guano, and built elaborate dovecotes for them so they would hang around and fertilize the banks of the Nile. Matisse gave Picasso a gift of pigeons, which inspired Picasso to draw his famously beautiful dove of peace. And think of Marlon Brando breaking down in tears in *On the Waterfront* when he discovered that his beloved pigeons had been viciously murdered in their rooftop coop.

Another quality of the pigeon is that it mates for life. That guttural cooing I'd heard from the pair on my terrace was their marriage song. Unbeknownst to me, the male had previously toured the area, scouting for a likely nesting site. He spotted my planter, with its dense, overhanging shrubs; a perfect nest really, shielded from rain and wind and almost hidden from the sight of predators. When he and his intended arrived at my terrace on that July day, he was showing her the real estate, asking whether she approved the proposed nest. Their mating depended on it. Evidently she was pleased, and only then, around the corner of the terrace, did they perform the ritual ceremony of their alliance: they cooed, they entwined their beaks in a kind of kiss, during which the male gave the female the gift of some regurgitated food, which assured her that he would help provide for their offspring. Only then did she allow him to do the deed, the work of mere seconds. A week later I found her eggs in the nest.

Last summer was long and hot. Heat wave followed heat wave. I kept the door to the terrace wide open late into the evening. Whatever I was doing—working at my desk, reading near the open door, pottering around the apartment, watering the tomatoes, I was constantly aware of the essential business of life going on a few feet away. During the three weeks of incubation the pigeons took turns sitting on the eggs. The mother, slightly smaller than her mate, was on the late shift; she arrived at the nest at about 5:30 each afternoon, and sat all through the night. At about 10:30 in the morning the father arrived to spell her, and sat until she returned in late afternoon.

Several times a day I pushed the shrubs aside to get a better view of what was going on in the nest. The female was imperturbable, but the male was skittish, hopping off the eggs when I came near. After a while he took me for granted. One very hot day he allowed me to come close enough to place a bowl of water beside him. He drank at once, then plopped himself into the bowl for a bath. It's ridiculous how happy that made me. Then, one afternoon, the hawk I often saw soaring high overhead, swooped down to land on the railing next to the nest. My god, he was gorgeous! Huge! A top-of-the-food-chain raptor! He turned his head toward me. I looked into his golden eyes and saw prehistory, I saw contempt. But he had not come to thrill me, he had come for my tasty pigeons. I shrieked at him. I shrieked again. Not worth the trouble, he must have thought, and showed me the breathtaking span of his wings as he took off.

Jenny has a tender feeling for pigeons. Not so much for the pigeon per se, but for the lullaby her mother sang each night to little Jenny and her big sister, Amy. Jenny sang it for me:

I open up my pigeon house
And set my pigeons free.
They fly around on every side
Till they perch on the highest tree.

And when they return from their merry merry flight
They close their eyes and they say goodnight.
Coo coo, coo coo, coo coo, etc.

One day Jenny came to town to see how my pigeons were doing. We sat on my sunny terrace, drinking iced tea, pots of flowering plants all around us, watching the placid father pigeon incubating his eggs, while Jenny told me a story.

At a party in her new town she'd met some other refugees from the city. They grouped together, as displaced people do, to talk about the old days in the old country—the days when they were young and starting out, the days before their cherished neighborhoods had been erased by gleaming designer buildings. They reminisced about the seventies and eighties, when the city had been a grubby paradise for the young and impecunious, full of cheap restaurants where you could eat a three-course meal for three dollars, where there was a bodega and a shoemaker on every street, where you could *always* find an affordable apartment or, better yet for an artist like Jenny, a huge, crumbling loft space where you could live and work. It's true that it was a city where the garbage piled up for days, even weeks, and

66

where you were likely to be mugged, but also a city that provided plenty of jobs for those with some basic skills—teaching gigs, handyman jobs—that supported life in those then-marginal neighborhoods where only hedge fund managers can afford to live today.

A man spoke up. "Yes," he said, "actually, Jenny Snider once told me that Philip Glass did the plumbing in her loft on Greenwich Street."

"No," said Jenny, "Philip Glass did the plumbing in the building next door."

The man was affronted. "How is it," he asked this new acquaintance, "that *you* feel able to speak with authority on this matter?"

"*I'm* Jenny Snider," said Jenny. "Who are you?"

He pronounced his name. They looked at each other closely, quizzically. Could it *be*? The years peeled away like the layers of an onion, their faces resumed youthful contours, gray hair turned dark . . . yes, yes, it might have been . . . it *had* been! They blushed.

Once upon a time they had known each other. Not for very long; not long enough to call what had passed between them an affair, just long enough for it to have been a *thing*. "I had a thing with her," is what he would have said when her name came up.

Jenny told me his name. Did I remember this guy?

I did. There had been no shortage of such guys in those footloose days when the heart was our only disposable property. Oh! the nervous excitement we'd felt when these things began: Would the guy call again? Would he turn out to be *the* guy? Jenny and I were privy to each other's tears in those days and, my god, what a river of them we'd shed when it became clear that our mothers had been right to instruct us that easy come meant easy go.

But look! Life had now offered Jenny an unexpected treat. She'd forgotten all about this guy, forgotten her tears, forgotten even his name. But she had remained in his life: lovely Jenny Snider, the girl with the gray eyes and long, curly black hair, the girl who could dance the night away and wake up in the morning to make art in her loft on Greenwich Street where Philip Glass had hooked up her sink and toilet; the girl who had told him that story, which became part of the repertoire of stories on which he dined out when the subject of the old days came up, the days when we had been young, a life condition that despite much confusion, frequent heartbreak, and disappointment was what we were *meant* to be. *Not* to be young? Unthinkable. *Impossible*. Yet here we were: without ever thinking the unthinkable, we had negotiated the impossible. Two gray-haired ladies sat on the terrace that life had granted one of them, drinking tea, talking about the old days, contemplating the pigeon, just as they were meant to do.

The chicks hatched in the third week of July. Hideous naked creatures, like dinosaur fetuses, with huge flesh-colored beaks and blind bulging eyes. Several times a day one or another parent took turns feeding them. With milk. It turns out that pigeons make milk; rich, curdy stuff that develops in the gullets of the mother *and* the father just days before the chicks hatch.

When they weren't eating, the chicks slept, curled into each other so closely that they looked like a dirty rag. Day by day they changed. Yellow fuzz began to cover their nakedness, spikes poked out of their bodies, threadlike feathery stuff developed on the spikes. After a while they began to stand up; like toddlers on their first legs they moved their pitiable winglike structures up and down. By the end of the third week they were fully feathered in slate gray. Now the mother seemed to be gone from their lives; only the father came to feed them, staying near the nest for hours, on guard. Soon the chicks began walking out of the nest to stand on the ledge. One day they flapped a short distance to my neighbor's ledge. They stood there for a few minutes looking stunned, then flapped back to the nest. Except that they still had no markings on their feathers, they had become indistinguishable from full-grown pigeons. And now that they had found their wings, they began to take longer trips. Some days they were gone for hours.

Early one morning, toward the end of August, I checked the nest. They were asleep. When I came home in the afternoon, they were gone, out for their daily jaunt, I assumed. They didn't come back. They'd flown the coop, their time had come.

Suppose you saw me on the street. Would you recognize me right off? I've let my hair go gray; and despite two, sometimes three, weekly trips to the gym, plus giving up dessert, a few more pounds have attached themselves to me. When I catch sight of my reflection in a shop window I think I must be in disguise. Here's a clue for you: There's a lady on 100th Street who mutters to the pigeons pecking on the ground. She says things like: *Hey guys, it's me. You know where I live. I have a nice place for you to nest.* She says: *Come home.*

Julie

I LOVE TOMATOES. All through the winter I'm comforted by thoughts of late July, when the first New Jersey tomatoes will arrive at the market and I'll eat them like apples, but with a little bit of salt. When tomato time is over I cook with the best and most expensive brand of canned tomatoes, the San Marzanos. All this being so, it seems strange to me that we'd been together for two or three months before you uttered the name of that fruit. It may be that during those months I said something like: "Isn't this a good tomato sauce?" and you simply agreed. Then one day I said impatiently: "I *wish* I could find some good tomatoes."

And you said: "It's not *tomahto* season yet."

I laughed. I thought you were making a joke.

I still had so much to learn.

For one thing, before I met you, I paid no attention to men's clothes. Women's clothes, yes of course. A woman can be transformed by a beautiful dress, turn heads when she walks into a room. No man can do that by virtue of what he wears. I always thought that one tweed jacket was pretty much like every other, and the same was true of men's suits, pants, shirts, and shoes. Men's clothes were no big deal.

I was about to be enlightened. *Your* tweed jackets, you would have me know, were the epitome of the genre, the product of numerous consultations with your tailor at Huntsman & Sons of Savile Row, with whom you debated the qualities of various Scottish and Irish tweeds, and who had then made your jackets precisely to your size and specifications. As for your shirts, tailors at Turnbull & Asser of Jermyn Street had made them to your measure from your choice of fabric. Your shoes? Handstitched by Cleverley & Co. in the Burlington Arcade, especially for the idiosyncrasies of your size-twelve tootsies. All was British, all was bespoke, all had been accumulated on your father's dime during your halcyon years as a ne'er-do-well abroad.

No doubt it was while chasing girls in London that you picked up the tomahto.

*

Just as it happens in the movies, the pages of the calendar flipped by. Our summers piled up, tomato seasons came and went, winter came, and the time came for you to sit down, never to rise again. As you knew better than anyone, only a standing man can present a *bella figura*. Your brilliant wardrobe hung, unworn, in the dark closet. And here's where I have to hand it to you: one night, when Alex came to dinner, you opened the closet door to him. Without a whimper, without a single complaint, with gaiety even, you offered up the raiment of your old life. Alex was delighted. *Everything*, even your shoes, fit him to a tee. He looked dashing, smashing as they say in England; he took those clothes back into the world they had been made for.

In any case, in those years we were much too busy with the latest medical news to worry about clothes. We had to follow up on stories of miraculous cures for multiple sclerosis, most of which seemed to be somewhere over the rainbow. We had neurologists to see, new drugs to try. We had to discuss the efficacy of the hyperbaric oxygen chamber; of having all your blood taken out, cleaned, and put back in again; we had to check out rumors of the curative power of drinks derived from the bark of birch trees that grew only in the remotest sites of Siberian gulags. And in the meantime, until any of these miracles were shown to be the least bit effective, there were mechanical devices to test—wheelchairs that took direction from your thoughts, software for the computer that would translate the spoken word to the screen, reading stands that could turn the pages of a book. Those reading stands were the *biggest* disappointment. Wouldn't you think that the simple, physical gesture of a finger turning a page could be mechanically replicated?

Then we heard about a new device. A steel suit, which was comparable to full body armor, or putting a skeleton outside your body. The point was that this iron suit-brace would keep you on your feet, while also somehow propelling your legs: you would "walk," as the literature put it.

What to do? Would this be yet another hideously expensive chase after another wild goose? We'd been disappointed so often, and we were *so* tired. Well, okay, but this would be our last hurrah, and with a huge effort we got ourselves to New Orleans. I'd never been to New Orleans. Such a beautiful city everyone said; so much to do, see, and eat. In our hotel room, we watched a thriller with Glenn Close and Jeff Bridges, and ate a room-service dinner. The next morning we saw the medical center where you were measured with even more precision than the best of your British tailors. And two months later your final bespoke suit arrived in New York, accompanied by the two strong men who were needed to get you into it. Funny; nobody had mentioned two strong men as a necessary accessory. But on this day at least, we had their services. In the time it would take to dream it, the strong men got you to your feet. You stood. The "walking" part? That never happened. Your physical deficits had hurried to outpace the usefulness of this device.

Still, it wasn't a total loss. I have a copy of the Polaroid taken by one of those men, and here we are standing side by side. At that moment I closed my eyes and nestled my head into the hollow of your shoulder, and you embrace me and smile very tentatively into the camera. "Look," you said when the Polaroid developed, "we could pass for a normal couple."

Calendar pages keep on flipping, it can't be helped. And when the page turned to the new millennium we found ourselves standing at edge of the valley of death. First to fall was your dear friend Vincent, then Frank, then Edward. Your turn came; a few months later it was Ernst, and a year after that, Christopher, and the next year, Alex.

I think about all of them, but when I think of Alex, I nurse a special fantasy. That one day I'll be rummaging around in one of those thrift shops where, to your great annoyance, I always bought my clothes, and I'll come upon a familiar-looking tweed jacket; I'll look at the label, which reads *Huntsman & Sons Ltd*. And the name of the man who bespoke it: *B. Sonnenberg 5.6.69*.

You have to admit that bespoke is a funny word. Did you ever conjugate it? If you plan to order custom-made clothes in the future, you have to say: "I will bespoke." Future perfect: "I will have bespoked." Past: "I bespoked." So, for instance, if I wanted to refer to the origin of my yellow terrycloth bathrobe, on which the name "Julie" was stitched in blue thread on the toweling, I'd have to say, "Julie bespoked it." Or is it "bespeaked"?

Not your sort of bespoke. Julie only ordered her name to be stitched on a mass-market robe. And then, for some reason, maybe because she hated wearing yellow, she donated that perfectly good robe to Goodwill, where one day I came upon it, and bought it for $4.99.

I said, "I hate wearing yellow, but this robe has years of use in it." And you said, "If you say so, Julie." So every Saturday morning, after we had coffee, I'd put on Julie's robe. We'd get you into the shower, and every Saturday morning, as the sun streamed through the east window, and the hot water poured down on us, and the bathroom filled with steam, I sang you this Jessi Colter song:

> I'm not Lisa, my name is Julie,
> Lisa left you years ago
> My eyes are not blue
> But mine won't leave you
> Till the sunlight has touched your face.

Mea Culpa

You never reproach me anymore, I have to do everything myself.

So, okay, I apologize for Daisy. I knew she wasn't the dog for you. You liked your dogs medium-to-large, wire-haired, terrierish, square-faced, willful. You liked a dog with a mind of its own, a dog who decided which commands to obey, which cushions and books required mastication, which hours of the day and night were most suitable for taking the air; and, once on the streets, which way to pull. That was Harry. He wasn't no trouble, as you would cheerfully agree.

You have to give me this much: after eleven years with Harry, I needed a vacation from that sort of dog—from all dogs, really. Whatever else you say about them, dogs control your life. But, *oh*, how you grieved for Harry! And, how empty our apartment felt without his animating presence. I thought cats might do the trick. You resigned yourself.

I went to Bideawee to shop for two cats. I would not even *look* at the door of the dog room for fear of a glimpse of pleading eyes. But in the cat room, what should I see? Two small black creatures in the same cage, only one of them a cat.

What is *this*?

It was the conceit of the cat-room keeper that the little black dog and cat were sisters. They had lived their short lives together, their owner had disposed of them together, and only together would they leave the orphanage. They had names: the dog was Angel, the cat Bones. There were plenty of other cats to choose from, but I picked up green-eyed Bones. She nestled in the hollow of my shoulder and started her motor. Yes, this was my cat. Then, of course, I had to pick up the importuning dog; she went wild with joy. She was so small, barely a dog at all, how much trouble could she be? And the truth is that once I'd picked her up I couldn't, could *not*, put her back into the cage.

They were young, under a year old, weighing less than ten pounds each; it would take three of both to make one Harry. I brought them home. I thought, I *hoped*, that you'd be so gladdened to have Harry's species in the house again that Angel, whose new name we debated, would disarm you. If not, I would pretend surprise: *Oh! You mean she's not a cat?* But I saw the look on your face when you first laid eyes on her: dismay, disappointment; and not only in the dog, in me: *My wife doesn't understand me. She thought I could be happy with this . . . this dogette!* But it was too late. I couldn't return her. Bideawee is not Bloomingdale's. Anyway, *I* was smitten.

She was such a little beauty. Her silky black hair brushed the floor; her long feathered ears hung like folded wings, until she pricked them, and then they stood straight up adding six inches to her height. Her long curled and feathered tail was always held high, her bright black, slightly bulging spaniel eyes were full of mischief. She didn't walk, she pranced. She was a French girl, a Papillon, a butterfly, a real breed. Or, more precisely, she was a moth—a Phalène, the drop-eared variety of the breed. As with so many girls, much of her beauty resided in her copious hair; when caught in a downpour or given a bath, she looked more like *une rate*.

I tried to raise her stock with you. In a book of sixteenth-century paintings I found her, surrounded by royalty: "Look at this!" I said, pointing to the little dog included in a portrait of Louis XIV *en famille*. And *look!* Titian had painted her, Renoir had painted her, Goya had painted her. It was said that Marie Antoinette had been so devoted to her Phalène that she took the little darling with her as she rode to the guillotine.

I know. You never did love her, but you came to not dislike her. She was amusing, chasing Bones through the rooms and rearing back in surprised offense when the cat batted her nose. When it snowed, she dashed in ecstatic circles, "like a crazy person," you said. She could do things Harry couldn't: she could jump up on the bed and make her nest between your legs. You got over the humiliation of being seen in public with a lady's lapdog, and took her on your lap on excursions to Riverside Park, and as far east as Central Park where she could run leash-free. She never ventured too far from you, she was the very model of obedience, always coming when called, sitting and staying when asked, alert, panting for play.

She loved the lap, but she would leap off in a moment to confront danger. She was without fear. She pranced up to Dobermans and Great Danes like the prettiest girl at the party, her head tilted high for a good sniff; if the big boys made an aggressive move, she nipped at their legs, barked hard, and ran them off. And the moment she understood the boundaries of her territory, she took up her life's work as a guard dog. She would not tolerate trespassers in the apartment, and she was always on duty. These trespassers thought they were our guests. She barked at them incessantly; even when we resorted to an electric dog collar that produced a shock at each bark, she barked on, if more hoarsely. *That* was annoying.

But her worst offense was not being Harry. Daisy was what she was, a frivolous girl, without gravitas, an accessory of a dog. Harry had been the dog of your heart, your pal, your confidant; in the deep hours of night you told him what you never told anyone else. And when you spoke to him, Harry's gaze never left you: he listened hard, he cocked his head to better take in your words. And when you had had your say, and asked him, "So what do you think about that, Har?" he licked your hand. He understood. Daisy had no patience for conversation. If you so much as looked at her, she'd leap up and dance on your lap. You couldn't tell that dog anything.

Sometimes you quoted Turgenev to me: "Oh well, a

man knows only so many dogs in his life." Sometimes you quoted Alexander Pope:

> Not louder shrieks to pitying Heav'n are cast,
> When husbands or when lap-dogs breathe their last.

Lapdogs live a long time. Sixteen years after I brought her home, Daisy died. I shed a few quiet tears, but not a single shriek for the lapdog did you hear from me. You missed the shrieks for the husband that came five months later. And in the midst of that grief, I thought about something you once wrote: "However I died, I was sure there would be a dog there at the end."

Bones

MAYBE YOU'D LIKE TO KNOW what happened to Bones. Of course you took the position that you didn't care for cats, but when Bones leapt into your lap anyone could see that you loved her.

For me Bones was perfect in kind and degree. She was a classic beauty in the way of sleekly black, green-eyed cats; and also, or foremost, she had a serene, affectionate nature. She liked to be brushed, she let me cut her nails, she even allowed children to pick her up. Whenever I called her name, she called in answer and bounded to my side. She liked to sit on laps, she liked to be stroked, she always used her litter box, she made no excessive demands for attention. Our Bones was no trouble.

When Daisy died she didn't seem to notice. I didn't blame her. The disappearance of a noisy, harassing rival is no cause for distress. When you died, I didn't notice whether she noticed.

For five months it was just me and Bones. Those first weeks are a blank to me. I must have fed her, cleaned her litter box, brushed her, cut her nails, but I don't remember. I don't remember if she hid herself on those nights when I went howling through the empty rooms. And when I knew that I couldn't go on living in our apartment, I must have put her in her carrier, taken her to my office, and lugged her up the four flights of stairs, but I have no memory of that either. Nor do I remember that she gave any signs of anxiety at being plucked from her home of a lifetime. She sniffed around that one-room-plus-kitchenette, found the perimeters, and settled in as though there had been no great life-changing event. She ate as usual, she never failed to use her litter box.

And between us, in that small room, we worked out the routine of our days. Every morning, at 7:30 on the dot, Bones meowed to wake me. I fed her, made my coffee, and read the paper. By 8:30 I was at my desk. While I worked she dozed in the wicker chair next to the sunny window, instantly alert at the appearance of a low-flying bird.

In the afternoons I went out to shop and do errands. I was always back by five o'clock to feed Bones. Friends were attentive to me in those early months; two or three nights a week I went out to dinner. On the other nights I fed Bones at the usual time, then prepared my own dinner. Not that I did any cooking at first, just heated up frozen dinners; later on I cooked spaghetti, or a hamburger.

After dinner it was my turn for the wicker chair. Bones sat on my lap while I read, or watched television. At eleven o'clock I went to the bathroom to brush my teeth, and she stretched herself and moved to her place on the futon. Every night I fell asleep grateful for her warm, purring weight. In this way we went through that first summer and fall together. She was only a cat; she wouldn't have done for you, but I felt companioned.

Then it was over. Early on a cold morning toward the end of November, I woke to see her staggering around the room.

Bones!

She didn't seem to hear. She staggered on blindly until her head hit the wall. Then she collapsed and lay unmoving, as flat as a wrung-out mop. As I had done with Daisy, less than a year before, I wrapped her in a towel and took her to the vet. Massive stroke, said the vet.

I stayed on in that room for another six or seven months. How I missed her, the comfort of her presence. I saw that I had fancied us as castaways on an island, lone survivors of a shipwreck. We had lived on board together, she knew what I knew.

DOROTHY GALLAGHER's works include two volumes of memoir—*How I Came into My Inheritance* and *Strangers in the House*—as well as a biography of the Italian American anarchist Carlo Tresca and, most recently, *Lillian Hellman: An Imperious Life*. She lives in New York.